MARK TWAIN

SUSAN BIVIN ALLER

In Consultation with Martha Cosgrove,
M.A. and Reading Specialist

JUST THE FACTS BIOGRAPHIES

LERNER PUBLICATIONS COMPANY / MINNEAPOLIS

Martha Cosgrove has a master's degree from the University of Minnesota in secondary education, with an emphasis on developmental and remedial reading. She is licensed in 7–12 English and language arts, developmental reading, and remedial reading. She has had several works published, and she gives numerous state and national presentations in her areas of expertise.

Lerner Publications Company
A division of Lerner Publishing Group
241 First Avenue North
Minneapolis, Minnesota 55401 U.S.A.

Website address: www.lernerbooks.com

Library of Congress Cataloging-in-Publication Data

Aller, Susan Bivin.
    Mark Twain / by Susan Bivin Aller.
       p.   cm. – (Just the facts biographies)
    Includes bibliographical references (p.   ) and index.
    ISBN-13: 978-0-8225-3425-9 (lib. bdg. : alk. paper)
    ISBN-10: 0-8225-3425-8 (lib. bdg. : alk. paper)
    1. Twain, Mark, 1835–1910–Juvenile literature. 2. Authors, American–19th century–Biography–Juvenile literature. I. Title. II. Series.
PS1331.A76 2006
818'.409–dc22   2005016780

Manufactured in the United States of America
1 2 3 4 5 6 – BP – 11 10 09 08 07 06

Contents

CHAPTER 1

BORN EXCITED

(Above) **This photo of Sam Clemens shows him as a printer-in-training. He would later be known as Mark Twain.**

THE TWELVE-YEAR-OLD red-haired boy stood on a wooden box. He was reaching for some metal printer's letters, but he was a bit too short. His secondhand clothing was too big. The boy chewed on a cigar and sang cheerfully as he worked.

This is how the writer Mark Twain remembered himself as a boy in 1848. At the time, he was working at a printer's shop in Hannibal, Missouri. He was not called Mark

Twain then. He was just plain Sam Clemens. He worked for a newspaper called the *Missouri Courier.*

One of his main jobs was setting type. This meant he set, or placed, metal letters, one by one. He put them into a Scrabble-like holder to make words. Then he arranged the words into sentences. (People with computers do this by typing and word processing.) Sam was quick at picking out the letters. He also cleaned up the office and delivered newspapers. Sam received no pay for his work, because he was an apprentice. As a printer's apprentice, he was learning to be a printer. His pay came in the form of being taught about printing. He also got food, a place to sleep, and two suits of clothes from the printer.

TYPESETTING, THEN AND NOW

In Sam's time, a printed page came from pieces of lead type that were set by hand. Each piece of type had a raised letter sticking out of it. Letters were lined up to make words. The words were lined up to make sentences. The sentences became pages. The hand-set type was inked. A machine pressed the inked typesetting onto a page. When the printing was finished, the letters were cleaned and put back in their storage boxes. Typesetting still takes place in modern newspapers, books, and magazines. But the process uses computers and laser printers instead of lead type placed one letter at a time.

This engraving shows Hannibal much as it was during Sam's childhood. Steamboats carried goods on the Mississippi River.

Sam liked his work. When he finished his apprenticeship, he'd be a printer. Sam decided he'd work for different newspapers so he could travel. But when the circus came to Hannibal, Sam thought that maybe he should be a clown. Clowns traveled too. Then an acting group arrived. Sam longed to be on stage with the actors.

He got his chance when he volunteered to be hypnotized by a traveling hypnotist. Sam only acted as if he were under the control of the hypnotist. He ran from imaginary snakes and kissed imaginary girls. He caught imaginary fish with an imaginary fishing pole. But then the hypnotist stuck Sam with pins. The man wanted to prove that Sam was truly hypnotized. The pins hurt! Sam had to pretend really hard that he couldn't feel them. Sam's acting made him famous for a week. Sam's next idea was that maybe he would become an actor. "I was born excited," he later wrote. Little did he know that during his life, he'd be a printer, a traveler, an actor, a clown—and much, much more.

EARLY CHALLENGES

Marshall Clemens, Sam Clemens's father, was a tall, stern man. He was respected for his honesty. His wife was Jane Clemens. The couple lived in Tennessee. By 1835, they had had four children— Orion, Pamela, Margaret, and Benjamin.

In Tennessee, Marshall had been a lawyer. Then he had run a small store. But he was not successful in either job. He lost most of his money and property. Then an invitation came from the Quarles family. Patsy Quarles was Jane's sister. Years before, Patsy and her husband John had moved westward to Florida, Missouri. They wrote glowing letters from Missouri. They urged Marshall and Jane to sell everything and join them there.

In the spring of 1835, the Clemens family got ready for the long, hard trip. Marshall and Jane Clemens were taking their four children from Tennessee to Missouri. It was a trip of more than 300 miles (480 kilometers).

Marshall loaded his family and goods into an old horse-drawn carriage. He and Jane rode in it with their three younger children—Pamela, Margaret, and Benjamin. Ten-year-old Orion rode on horseback. Hopes of success lay ahead.

John Quarles had asked Marshall to be a partner in his general store. Marshall Clemens would also open a new law office in Missouri. As the town's leading citizen, John was working to make the town grow. He wanted to attract steamboats and railroads and more settlers to it.

Marshall and Jane Clemens couldn't afford another child. But during the long westward trip to Missouri, Jane became pregnant again. The

Sam Clemens was born in this two-room house in Florida, Missouri, in 1835.

family reached Florida, Missouri, in the summer of 1835. The town had twenty log houses and about one hundred settlers. Marshall rented a simple two-room house. There, on November 30, the new baby arrived, two months early. In those days, early babies often didn't survive. That night, Halley's Comet streaked across the sky. Jane believed this was a good sign. Her tiny baby

IT'S A FACT!

Halley's Comet is named after a British scientist named Edmund Halley. Records of the comet stretch back to ancient times. The comet appeared in 1531, 1607, 1682, and 1758 before appearing in 1835, when Sam was born. It also appeared in 1910, when he died.

would live, and he would be special.

The parents named the new baby Samuel Langhorne Clemens. But the family called the baby Sammy or Little Sam. Sammy was weak and often sick. Jane was determined he'd make it. She gave him all kinds of homemade cures for his many illnesses. The medicines tasted terrible, but he did get stronger.

Marshall Clemens spent what little money he had to buy land. He planned to build a grand house in Florida. The town elected him a justice of the peace and called him Judge Clemens. Like John Quarles, Marshall became a leader in the town. But, unlike John, Marshall was not a good businessman. His partnership with John Quarles fell apart. His law practice didn't pay enough to support his family. Finally, all he could afford to build were two single-room cabins joined together.

In 1838, when Sam was nearly three, the Clemenses had another baby. They called him Henry. A year later, Sam's sister Margaret died of a sudden fever. By this time, Marshall Clemens was not succeeding as he'd hoped. The family was grief-stricken and poor.

MOVING TO HANNIBAL

Marshall was disappointed with his failures. He traded his property and much of his cash for some land in Hannibal, Missouri. This town was about thirty miles east on the banks of the Mississippi River.

Marshall and Jane Clemens arrived in Hannibal in 1839. They joined about sixty other farming families there. Most of the families raised hogs and grew crops such as wheat and tobacco. Hannibal was in a good spot. Barges and steamboats docked at Hannibal and carried goods to markets along the river. The town grew. Unpaved roads crossed the town. They climbed steeply away from the river into nearby fields and wilderness.

Marshall's piece of land was in the center of town. On it was a small hotel called the Virginia

House. Another building was turned into a store. He moved his family into the Virginia House. Then he borrowed money to buy goods. Orion, Sam's oldest brother, ran the store.

Sam continued to be the family's most excitable child. He sometimes walked in his sleep. Sometimes his family would find him in a dark corner, weeping with fear from nightmares. At the same time, Sam looked like an angel. He had thick reddish hair, a sweet smile, and innocent gray green eyes. He spoke in a slow way. His family called it "Sammy's long talk." But Sam's behavior was far from angelic.

Sam started school in 1840, when he was about five. He sometimes made trouble in class. But he became the school's best speller. Sam was a favorite with the girls because he was gentle with them and made them laugh. Sam and his young friends played in the woods outside of town. They dug for pirate treasure. They waded in the streams and fished. They collected turtle eggs and other fascinating things. Sam and his friends loved playing along the Mississippi. They pretended to be steamboats. They made clanging and hissing noises. They marched forward and then backward. This movement reminded them of how the huge boats came in and out of Hannibal.

Meanwhile, things were not going well with the Clemens family. Orion wasn't skilled at managing the store, and it failed. So Marshall sent his oldest son to work for a printer in Saint Louis, Missouri. Judge Clemens began to work as a lawyer again. In the spring of 1842, Sam's brother Benjamin died after a sudden illness. Six-year-old Sam looked on with shock as his mother wept by the dead boy's bed.

IT'S A FACT!

Once, when Sam's mother emptied his pockets, she found two fish hooks, a slingshot, marbles, a broken stick of chalk, and a wooden soldier with one leg.

2 A HEAVENLY PLACE FOR A BOY

THE CLEMENS FAMILY STRUGGLED. But the Quarles family was doing well. John Quarles had moved his large family to a farm just outside of Florida, Missouri. So, after Benjamin died, Jane took Sam, Pamela, and Henry to stay with Aunt Patsy and Uncle John on the Quarles farm. Sam would later call it, "a heavenly place for a boy."

For an entire summer, Sam found himself in a large and loving family. His aunt and uncle had eight children. Uncle John was a big, friendly man who joked with the children and told them stories. Aunt Patsy was a lively woman. Several slave families also lived on the farm. They helped harvest crops and take care of the house.

Aunt Patsy liked to bring together her large family for big meals on the huge covered porch. She and her slaves cooked fried chicken, roast pig, turkey, and rabbit. They baked biscuits and batter cakes. They boiled corn on the cob. Fresh fruits and vegetables were everywhere.

On the farm, Sam grew stronger and healthier. He roamed barefoot with his cousins. He explored the stables and learned to ride horses. He found out how to pick the sweetest watermelons. Sometimes Sam was allowed to go hunting at night. Slaves with torches would lead him and his cousins into the nearby forest. When the dogs barked, it meant that a small wild animal had run up a tree. Then everyone scrambled through the forest to get to the spot. They'd light a fire and chop down the tree to catch the animal.

SLAVE STORIES

Behind the farm's fruit orchard, Uncle John's slave families lived in small log cabins. Through the trees, Sam could see the lights of their fires and hear them singing. The families welcomed him whenever he visited. He felt safe and protected. He listened in wonder to the stories and music of the slaves. They came from many different homelands.

They spoke in a rich mixture of West African, British, Caribbean, and U.S. local languages. He listened to and remembered their songs and their way of telling stories.

Sam became close to gray-haired Uncle Dan'l. He headed one of the slave families. Uncle Dan'l was a warmhearted adviser and friend to all the children. But for Sam, in particular, he became a model for loyalty, kindness, and storytelling.

On special nights, Uncle Dan'l sat all the children—black and white—around his kitchen fire. He'd tell them stories. Some were magical. Others were funny. Some stories were very scary. Uncle Dan'l's voice rose and fell with each telling. When the fire had nearly burned out, the children huddled around Uncle Dan'l for the final story— the ghost story. "Once 'pon a time," it always began. The old man would weave his hands through the shadows and cry in the voice of the ghost "Who-o-o got my golden arm?" The children shivered with delight. They'd scream when he yelled out the last line. "YOU GOT IT!" Then the children went off to bed. Sam would leave and climb to his room in the main house.

He still heard "Who-o-o got my golden arm?" in his ears.

As Sam grew older and healthier, he caused more trouble and excitement. For example, he put garter snakes in Aunt Patsy's sewing basket "for a surprise." To his mother, Sam would say, "there's something in my coat pocket for you." She'd put in her hand and pull it right out with a shiver. A bat!

Sam sensed that, even with his pranks, he was probably his mother's favorite child. "I think she enjoyed it. She had no [trouble] at all with my brother Henry. . . . I think . . . his goodness and truthfulness and obedience would have been a

This portrait of Sam's mother, Jane Clemens, shows her at the age of fifty-five.

burden to her but for the relief [I gave her by behaving] in the other direction."

BACK IN HANNIBAL

After the summer, the Clemens family returned to Hannibal. Sam continued to tease his mother. He played hooky from school and lied when he was caught. He often tattled on his perfect brother Henry.

By the time he was ten, he'd become a serious troublemaker. He'd sneak out at night to meet his friends. Their leader was an older boy named Tom Blankenship, son of the town drunkard. Jane had forbidden Sam to play with Tom. But her rule just made the escape more exciting. Tom never had to go to school or take a bath or do any of the other things Sam had to do. Tom knew all about hunting

IT'S A FACT!

When Sam was nine years old, he hid on a steamboat and sailed down the Mississippi. He was soon discovered and was let off the boat at the next stop. Relatives took him back to his mother, who punished him. The punishment didn't cure Sam of his dream. He was sure he wanted to become a steamboat man when he grew up.

and trapping animals. He could ward off evil with spells and charms. He knew how to cure warts with dead cats.

A lot of the boys' nighttime adventures took place in the local cemetery. Tom had dreams that told him where to find buried treasure. He made the younger boys dig for it. As they worked, Tom leaned against a tree, smoking a pipe. Sam's closest friend, though, was Will Bowen. Together, the two played Robin Hood and pirates in caves above the river.

Hannibal was a young, rough frontier town. Sam saw crimes and violent acts on the streets. He saw the cruelty of slavery. The slaves Sam knew on Uncle John's farm were treated well.

THE MISSOURI COMPROMISE

In the 1800s, the United States was a growing nation. New states were being added as the country expanded westward. Slavery was still legal at this time. But states had opposing views about slavery. So the U.S. Congress tried to keep the number of new states that allowed slavery (called slave states) the same as the number that didn't allow slavery (free states). Missouri wanted to join the United States as a slave state. Before it could do so, it had to be paired with a free state. Maine (free state) and Missouri (slave state) became U.S. states in 1820. The law that paired them was called the Missouri Compromise.

But he knew slavery wasn't fair. On the streets of Hannibal, he saw a slave die after his owner hit him with a rock. Sam was sickened when he saw a group of black men and women chained together and lying on the pavement. They were waiting to be shipped down the river to be sold at a slave market.

LURED BY THE RIVER

The long and wide Mississippi River thrilled and scared Sam. He knew that people could easily drown in it. Two of Sam's friends had lost their lives swimming in the river. Sam himself was rescued from drowning twice, once by a man and once by a girl, both slaves. His frightened mother comforted herself by saying there wasn't much danger for a boy as troublesome as Sam. "People who are born to be hanged are safe in the water," she joked.

Sam and his friends often swam out into the river to get a ride on a boat floating downstream to New Orleans, Louisiana. Sam was fascinated by the rude manners and bad language of the crews. He watched the boasting, brawling, drunken boatmen and listened to their loud yells.

Showboats brought excitement, traveling entertainment, and business to towns along the Mississippi River.

His favorite boats were steamboats. Most carried goods and passengers. Others were dressed up as showboats. These boats brought singers, dancers, and bands to towns along the river. They also brought gamblers and con artists. Actors, magicians, mind readers, and circus performers came and went with the showboats. Sam saw every bit of this colorful flow of people.

IT'S A FACT!

A musical play, named *Show Boat*, opened in 1927. Movie versions came out in 1929, 1936, 1946, and 1951. The play and the movies capture the sounds and excitement of a showboat arriving at a Mississippi town.

The wharf (landing) at Hannibal was usually quiet. But when the cry "steamboat-a-comin!" rang out, the town came alive. Sam later described it. "Carts, men, boys, all go hurrying from many quarters to . . . the wharf. . . . The people fasten their eyes upon the coming boat as upon a wonder they are seeing for the first time. . . . The . . . upper decks are [filled] with passengers; the captain stands by the big bell, calm, imposing, the envy of all." After a few minutes of extreme noise and activity, passengers and freight were unloaded and loaded. "The steamer is under way again. . . . After ten more minutes the town is dead again."

When Sam was eleven, his father got a lung disease called pneumonia. Jane called Orion back from his printer's job in Saint Louis. Two weeks later, with his family at his bedside, Marshall Clemens died. He was forty-eight. Sam remembered, "He put his arm around my sister's neck and kissed her. . . . In all my life, up to that time, I had never seen one member of the Clemens family kiss another one."

CHAPTER 3
TOOLS OF THE TRADE

AFTER HIS FATHER'S DEATH, Sam promised his mother he'd try to behave better. But both mother and son knew the odds weren't good that he could keep that promise for long. He wanted to be serious and hardworking, but he just couldn't help being quirky and troublesome.

Tougher times were ahead. Marshall Clemens had left little money behind. It soon became clear to Jane and Orion that the family needed money quickly. Orion went back to Saint Louis. At the printer's, he earned enough to send home three dollars a week. Pamela earned money by giving guitar and piano lessons. Jane took in boarders, who paid her money for a room and meals.

BEING A PRINTER

In 1848, when Sam was twelve, he was sent to Joseph Ament's shop to be a live-in apprentice. Ament owned Hannibal's newspaper, the *Missouri Courier*. Sam would learn the printer's trade there. At Ament's shop, Sam learned how to hand-set words. This task involved lining up individual letters of metal type. Sam's good spelling helped him to work accurately. He weighed the metal words in his hands. He started to feel how much weight would fit into a form to become sentences on printed pages. He also learned that the quicker a printer turned out pages of type, the more money he earned.

IT'S A FACT!

The *Missouri Courier* was hooked up to a new technology called the telegraph. Telegraph wires were strung between poles across the country. Messages were sent over the wires by typing words into a machine at one end. At the other end, another machine received the news. This way, news traveled quickly. As a result, Hannibal had a fast link to the outside world. In 1848, the United States was just finishing a war against Mexico. Sam set type for battlefield stories fresh from the telegraph.

Sam lived and worked as an apprentice for two years in a print shop much like this one.

Sam and the other apprentices slept on the office floor. When they didn't get enough to eat, they'd sneak down to the cellar for potatoes and onions. The boys would cook them on the office stove.

Sam still got into mischief. The upstairs window of the printing shop offered a fine view of the street. One day, Sam saw his perfect little brother, Henry, passing by. Sam had an urge to drop a watermelon shell on Henry's head. It was "a thing which I have been trying to regret for fifty-five years," he later wrote.

Toward the end of Sam's apprenticeship, Orion moved back to Hannibal. He borrowed money and bought his own newspaper. When his apprenticeship ended, Sam went to work for his brother.

A NEW THIRST

One day, Sam was walking along the street. He reached down to pick up a piece of paper. It was the page of a book about Joan of Arc. Sam knew almost nothing about history. He had never heard of the French girl who had led a French army to victory in the 1400s. The story of her heroism moved him. He borrowed a book about Joan of Arc. From that moment on, he studied history whenever he could.

JOAN OF ARC

Joan is a French hero from the 1400s. She never went to school, and she was a serious Roman Catholic. She believed that God had sent her to lead the French army in battle against the English army. She and the French beat the English in battle at the city of Orléans, France. Joan became known as the Maid of Orléans. New Orleans, the US city at the end of the Mississippi River, is named after this French city.

The more he read, the more he wanted to read. He began to study German. His reading gave him ideas for articles and stories. He asked Orion if he could write some for the paper. Orion agreed. But the Hannibal paper was small. Only a small group of people read it. Sam wanted more people to read what he wrote. So he wrote some articles about Hannibal for newspapers in Boston, Massachusetts, and in Philadelphia, Pennsylvania. He was thrilled when they were printed over his initials "S.L.C." He was sixteen years old, and two big-city newspapers had paid him for his writing!

Orion sometimes went out of town on short business trips. Every time, he left Sam in charge of the paper. Sam took the chance to use his talent for storytelling and humor to liven up the paper. For example, he created a large headline that read, "Terrible Accident! 500 men killed and missing!!!" Underneath, Sam had printed in smaller type, "We had set the above . . . , expecting (of course) to use it, but as the accident hasn't happened, yet, we'll say (To be Continued)." The paper's subscribers liked the change. The number of people buying the paper went up during Orion's absences.

By the spring of 1853, seventeen-year-old Sam was tired of working for his brother. Orion couldn't afford to pay Sam a salary. Even though Sam was now a printer, he was still working as if he were an apprentice. He wanted to get away.

IT'S A FACT!

New subscribers to Orion's paper often paid in turnips and wood instead of in cash.

He told his mother he was going to Saint Louis to work as a paid printer for a few months. He would stay with his sister Pamela. She had recently married a successful merchant named Will Moffett. But Sam's real goal was to go to New York City. He wanted to see the Crystal Palace, which was the main building of a new exhibition. After two months in Saint Louis, he headed for New York.

EARLY TRAVELS

While he was in New York, Sam worked in a printing office. In the evenings, he read at a library. By early October, Sam was ready to move on. He worked night shifts in Philadelphia for a while. Then he headed to Washington, D.C.

NEW YORK'S CRYSTAL PALACE

The building that Sam was so interested in seeing was part of the Great Exhibition of Art and Industry of 1853. Held in New York, this huge exhibit showed the newest and best accomplishments in painting, mining, photography, and sculpture. New inventions were also part of the show.

The main exhibit area was the Crystal Palace. Shaped like a cross, the palace had three grand entrances. Towers stood at the end of each arm of the cross. Over the top was a huge glass dome that reached 125 feet (38 meters) high. About 15,000 panes of glass covered the building. More than 5,000 exhibitors from the United States and many foreign countries set up exhibits. The building burned down in 1857.

The Crystal Palace

After a year away from his family, Sam returned for a visit.

While Sam was away, Orion had sold his Hannibal newspaper. He had moved to Muscatine, Iowa, where he ran another newspaper. He had taken his mother and Henry to live with him. Soon afterward, Orion married and moved to his wife's hometown of Keokuk, Iowa. There, he bought

Sam spent several years working as a printer and traveling around the United States.

Orion (right), Sam's older brother, bought a newspaper. He convinced Sam to work for him.

another newspaper. Jane decided to leave the newlyweds alone. She went to Saint Louis to live with Pamela.

Orion needed cheap labor. He urged Sam and Henry to come work for him in Keokuk. They did, and Sam entertained himself there by taking dancing lessons and leading an active social life. He had a good singing voice, and he could play the piano and guitar fairly well. Young ladies liked his good looks and happy nature.

At a printers' banquet in Keokuk, Sam gave his first funny after-dinner speech. He began to tell jokes in his drawling "long talk," which he had first shown his family when he was a child. His fellow printers roared with laughter. For Sam, this was more fun than being on stage with the hypnotist!

In all, Sam spent about ten years as a printer. He saw different parts of the country. He met many kinds of people. He lived in boardinghouses and hotels. He sometimes went hungry and sometimes had enough to spend on luxuries. Most of all, Sam read and read and read. He read just about anything, including poetry, history, and geography. He read stories written for the newspapers he worked on. Sometimes, if a column ran short, he filled it out with stories of his own.

CHAPTER 4

PILOTING THE MISSISSIPPI

RESTLESS ONCE MORE, twenty-two-year-old Sam decided he would go to Brazil in South America. He'd heard it was easy to make a fortune there. In Cincinnati, Ohio, he boarded a steamship. It would take him part of the way along the Mississippi. Another ship would take him the rest of the way.

CONVINCING BIXBY

On the way down the river, Sam remembered his boyhood dream of working on a Mississippi steamboat. This dream focused on the pilot, who guided the ship up and down the river.

At the wheel of the steamship stood one of the great pilots of the river, Horace Bixby. Only nine years older than Sam, Bixby had a dozen years of experience. He was licensed to be a pilot on the Mississippi River. He had a quick temper and expected perfection from any cubs (pilot trainees) learning from him.

IT'S A FACT!

Ship pilots and ship captains are not the same thing. A ship's pilot is in charge of moving a ship safely through waters near a coast or riverbank. A ship's captain is in charge of the entire process of moving a ship, its cargo, and its passengers safely to its destination.

Horace Bixby was nursing a sore foot when Sam boarded his boat. Before long, Sam talked his way into the pilot's office. He helped steer while Bixby rested his foot. Bixby knew Will Bowen, Sam's boyhood friend from Hannibal. Will was piloting another steamboat on the river. Bixby respected Will, so Sam had an advantage.

"At the end of three hard days, [Bixby] surrendered. He agreed to teach me the Mississippi River from New Orleans to Saint Louis for five hundred dollars, payable out of the first wages I should receive after graduating. I entered upon the small enterprise of 'learning' twelve or thirteen hundred miles of the great Mississippi River with the easy confidence of my time of life. If I had really known what I was about to [get into], I should not have had the courage to begin."

LEARNING TO BE A PILOT

Instead of going to Brazil, Sam went back upriver. On the return trip from New Orleans to Saint Louis, Sam worked as the new cub. He wrote down thousands of details he would need to know to earn his pilot's license. These details included the names of islands and towns and the location of dangerous sandbars. He needed to remember how to guide a ship through each bend in the mighty river.

Sam was feeling quite smart about how much he knew. Then Bixby asked him the shape of a certain bend. Sam said he didn't know it had any particular shape. Bixby got really angry. Everything on the riverbanks had a shape, Bixby said. The only way a pilot could tell his location was to learn the shape by heart. A good pilot had to know the bends in daylight and at night, in full moonlight and in a thick mist. Only a pilot's memory of it would get him by safely.

Steamboats also needed to keep clear of the shallow parts of the river. If a boat ended up in less than 9 or 10 feet (3 meters) of water, it would hit bottom and get stuck. A stuck boat was tough to get going again. If a sailor yelled "mark twain," it meant the depth of the river was 12 feet (3.7 meters). This was the boundary between water deep enough and water too shallow for a steamboat. Hearing "mark twain" was a warning to head for deeper, safer water.

RIVER DEPTHS

At this time, no electronic instruments existed to help figure out the depth of a river. But sailors used an age-old method. They dropped lead lines into the water. These lines were long ropes with a lead weight at the end. Lead lines helped sailors get a measurement of how deep the water was.

Colored cloth on the lead line marked each fathom (every 6 feet). Sailors would call out the depth by seeing how many colored cloths were underwater. Deep four was 24 feet (7.3 meters). Mark three was 18 feet (5.4 meters). Half twain—between mark three and mark two—was 15 feet (4.5 meters). MARK TWAIN was 12 feet (3.7 meters). If the number of fathoms was going up from mark twain, the depth was enough for the steamboat. But if the numbers were at mark twain or below, the pilot had to be very careful.

Becoming a pilot took all the focus Sam had. Horace Bixby was a hard teacher. He was furious when his cub made mistakes. He roared at Sam, "When I say I'll learn a man the river, I mean it. And you can depend on it, I'll learn him or kill him." Sam nearly quit several times.

PILOT LIFE

Coal-burning furnaces, called boilers, create the steam to run steamboats. The boilers are very dangerous. No one could tell when a steamboat boiler might explode. The riverbed was littered with the broken remains of steamboats that had blown up. Most steamboats survived only four or five years.

Sam was finishing his first year of training when Bixby sent him to work with the pilot of the steamboat *Pennsylvania*. The pilot was a mean-tempered man named Brown. Sam had brought along his nineteen-year-old brother Henry. Henry was to work as a clerk on the same boat. Sam was pleased to see his brother starting on a promising career.

For some reason, Brown couldn't stand Sam. He eventually took out his anger on young

Henry. At one point, Brown threw a large lump of coal at Henry's head. Just in time, Sam ran between them with a heavy stool. He knocked Brown to the floor. He jumped on him and beat him. As a result of the fight, Sam was sent to another boat, but Henry remained with the *Pennsylvania.* Shortly afterward, the *Pennsylvania*'s boilers exploded. Henry was killed. Sam never forgave himself. He always felt partly responsible for Henry's death.

Sam and his younger brother, Henry (left), both worked on the Pennsylvania.

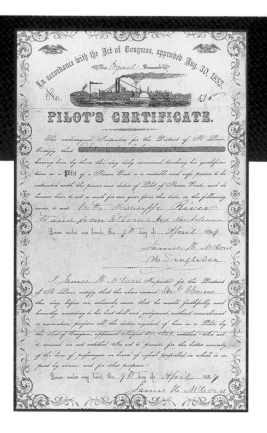

Sam earned his steamboat pilot's license in 1859.

Sam continued his training. In 1859, two years after he began training, Sam earned his pilot's license. He had learned the river.

Life as a pilot suited Sam perfectly. It was not dirty or physically hard. He began to wear spotless white trousers, a long blue jacket, and a fancy striped shirt. He grew side-whiskers to look more mature than his twenty-three years. And he brushed his unruly reddish hair high on top so he would appear taller.

A pilot earned a $3,000 year. (In modern money, this equals about $61,000.) In some jobs, $500 ($10,000) a year was normal. Sam felt he was being paid very well. Since he lived on the steamboat, he didn't have to pay rent or buy food. He could send money home to his mother as well as buy himself a few pleasures. And he never lost his love of being on stage. He liked telling stories and being funny. He liked sharing jokes with people.

Pilots gathered in social groups to hear Sam tell his funny stories. He continued to try out different ways to tell jokes. One approach was a slow, drawling, serious delivery. This style had begun when he was a child. It had worked well with his printer friends. Soon Sam became a favorite entertainer along the river.

All this time, Sam had kept on reading. He'd become a book fanatic. He spent hours learning French and reading history, travel, and science books. In English, he read the classic works of William Shakespeare, Sir Walter Scott, and John Bunyan. During his career, Sam would write a few classics himself.

THE CIVIL WAR

While Sam was enjoying his success, trouble was brewing in the United States. The issue was whether Southern U.S. states could own slaves. Northern states of the Union had outlawed slavery. Southern states feared that the right to own slaves would be taken away from them. So, in 1861, several slaveholding Southern states decided to separate from the Union. These states formed the Confederacy. Confederate troops fired on the Union's Fort Sumter in April 1861. This action started the Civil War (1861–1865). U.S. president Abraham Lincoln closed the Mississippi River to nonmilitary traffic. He wanted to stop supplies from getting to the South.

IT'S A FACT!

In the 1800s, most supplies and other cargo were shipped on boats. The Mississippi River was one of the main rivers for sending goods across the United States.

Sam's job as a pilot had taken him up and down the river, into the North and the South. When the war started, he couldn't decide which side to support. But, with river traffic closed, he couldn't remain on the river. Sam's career as a pilot was over.

Sam visited his mother and sister in Saint Louis. He went to see old school friends in Hannibal. They talked him into joining the Confederate cause. He became part of the Marion Rangers. The military group was named after Marion County, where Hannibal was located.

Politics in Missouri were confusing. Missouri was a slaveholding state. But it had remained part of the Union. Even so, Union troops might invade the state. Sam wasn't convinced that either side was right. Everyone thought the war would be over in a few months.

CHAPTER 5
LEAVING THE MIDWEST

LIEUTENANT SAMUEL CLEMENS was riding a stubborn mule called Paint Brush. Only a month earlier, Sam had been dressed like a gentleman. He had been in charge of a Mississippi steamboat. Because of the war, he had lost his comfortable life.

Local farmers had outfitted Sam and the other Marion Rangers for war. The Rangers would be on the Southern, or Confederate, side. They'd be fighting the troops of the North, or the Union. Each man got a mule and a rifle. They also got three blankets, a frying pan, a suitcase, an overcoat, some rope, and an umbrella.

SOLDIERING AND MORE TRAVELS

Starting from Hannibal, the Rangers moved only
at night. They needed to avoid Union patrols. The
Rangers headed for the town of Florida, where
they hoped to join the Confederate troops. But
people who sided with the North chased them
away. Heavy rains came. Nobody would obey
orders to stand guard in the rain. Finally, Sam had
to walk. He had developed a sore that made it
impossible to ride his mule.

Rumors said Union troops were heading
toward the Rangers. The small group retreated,
or pulled back. Sam wrote that he knew more
about retreating than the person who invented
retreating.

The Rangers slept in a hayloft one night. One
of the group set fire to the hay with his pipe. Sam
quickly rolled away from the fire. To escape, he
jumped out of a window, spraining his ankle.

By this time, the Marion Rangers had lost their
interest in army life. They broke up after only two
weeks. Sam stayed at a farmhouse until his sore
and ankle healed. He grew afraid that he'd be shot
for leaving the army without permission. He went
back to Iowa and hid at Orion's house.

In July 1861, the two brothers boarded a horse-drawn stagecoach for the long trip from Missouri to Nevada. There, Orion had a new job as secretary to the governor of Nevada Territory. Sam was to be Orion's secretary.

The stagecoach traded its tired horses for fresh ones every 10 miles (16 kilometers) of a trip that was more than 1,000 miles (1,609 kilometers). But the passengers were not given any time to change clothes or bathe. More than once, they were passed by a galloping Pony Express rider, who was carrying a precious packet of mail. The stagecoach arrived in Carson City, Nevada Territory. Sam and Orion had traveled almost nonstop for twenty days.

THE PONY EXPRESS

Twain wrote about the fast mail service called the Pony Express in a book called *Roughing It:*

> Every neck is stretched further, and every eye strained wider. Away across the endless . . . prairie a black speck appears against the sky, and it is plain that it moves. . . . In a second or two it becomes a horse and rider, rising and falling, rising and falling—sweeping toward us nearer and nearer—growing more and more distinct . . . sharply defined—nearer and still nearer, and the flutter of the hoofs comes faintly to the ear. . . . [A] man and horse burst past our excited faces, and go winging away like [the] fragment of a storm!

A WRITING JOB

Sam didn't have much work to do for Orion, so he looked for some excitement. He spent several months in the Sierra Nevada searching for silver and panning for gold. He invested in mines that miners swore were sure bets to make money. Sam went broke trying to strike it rich.

Sam shared a cabin with several fellow miners. At night, he wrote about his experiences. He sent

Many people moved west in search of gold in the mid-1800s. These three men are panning for gold by a stream.

his writings to a newspaper called the *Territorial Enterprise* in Virginia City and to other papers in Nevada and California. He signed these articles "Josh." But they didn't bring much money. Sam was seriously looking for a way to support himself.

Finally, Joseph Goodman, the editor of the *Territorial Enterprise,* offered Sam $25 (modern $500) a week to join his staff. Twenty-five dollars wasn't even close to a steamboat pilot's pay. But Sam was nearly penniless. He didn't have enough money to hire a horse. So he picked up his gear and walked the 130 miles (209 kilometers) from his mining camp to Virginia City.

On a hot day in September 1862, Sam limped into the newspaper's office. He dropped into a chair. He wore a faded flannel shirt with trousers tucked into his boots. A dirty hat covered his long reddish hair. His long beard was stained with dust He asked to see the editor. Who was this? the startled clerk wanted to know. "My name is Clemens, and I've come to write for the paper."

On February 3, 1863, six months after starting work on the *Enterprise,* Sam signed a funny travel article with the name Mark Twain. It stuck. People began calling him Mark Twain.

Sam first signed his name as Mark Twain on February 3, 1863, when he worked for the *Territorial Enterprise*. The newspaper's office is shown above.

Sam Clemens had certainly heard "mark twain" called out many times on the Mississippi River. He may have chosen it as his pen name because he liked the sound of it. Maybe it reminded him of the best job he had ever had.

This lithograph of Virginia City is borderd by images of the buildings in the town. The *Territorial Enterprise* office is shown on the top row, fourth from the right.

Sam loved wearing fancy clothes and being recognized on the streets of Virginia City. He had grown to be a young man of medium height. He was not very big and had narrow, sloping shoulders. He usually held a cigar in his rather delicate hands. His intense gray green eyes attracted people's attention. So did his thick eyebrows and unruly reddish hair. His social crowd was made up of rowdy, drinking, gambling writers and entertainers.

Eventually, Sam grew restless in the small town of Virginia City. He loved to visit San Francisco in nearby California. He liked its fine restaurants, hotels, and theaters. He moved to the city in 1864. He got a job on the *Morning Call* newspaper. He became friends with Steve Gillis, another reporter at the *Call*.

Soon Sam and Steve were in trouble for various pranks. They left town and went to look for gold in the Sierra foothills near Jackass Hill. Steve's two brothers had a cabin in the town. In good weather, Steve and Sam panned for gold in the foothills. They were hoping to wash a few gold nuggets free of the dirt into their pans. When the weather was bad, they sat around the fire and told stories or read books. Sam later spent four cold, wet weeks at a larger mining settlement called Angel's Camp. Even though he had no luck finding gold, he got something out of the experience. The stories and characters he found at Jackass Hill and Angel's Camp gave him writing ideas. One of his favorites was about a fellow named Jim Smiley, who had a jumping frog. (This idea later ended up in Sam's first book.)

VISITING HAWAII

Sam returned to San Francisco to work at the *Call.*
But he felt trapped there. Another paper wrote a
personal attack about Sam. He grew very
depressed. In October 1865, he wrote to Orion that
he was miserable.

Soon afterward, rescue came. The *Sacramento
Union*–a newspaper in northern California–asked
Mark Twain to write stories from Hawaii. The
Hawaiian Islands were not yet part of the United
States. They were ruled by a Hawaiian royal family.
A British explorer had named the islands the
Sandwich Islands. In 1866, supplied with cigars,
brandy, and introductions from friends, Sam left on
the steamship *Ajax.*

The eleven-day journey from San Francisco to
the Sandwich Islands gave Sam enough material for
his first articles for the *Union.* His idea was to stay
only a month. But he liked the islands and their
people. He stretched his visit to four months.

He wrote twenty-five travel articles. They
reached a wide audience. For the first time, many
readers learned about the natural beauty and
history of Hawaii. During a night visit to a live
volcano, Sam wrote that the inside of the volcano

Sam visited Hawaii in 1866.

"was as black as ink . . . but over a mile square of it was ringed and streaked and striped with a thousand branching streams of liquid and gorgeously brilliant fire!"

One day, word came that a lifeboat had landed on Hawaii. It was carrying fifteen starving men who had been at sea for forty-three days. They were survivors of a U.S. ship that had burned at sea. Sam interviewed the survivors in the hospital. He quickly wrote a story. Ships were the only link between the Sandwich Islands and the mainland.

The next morning, a messenger sent the article on a ship bound for the United States. (No telegraph was on the islands.) Sam's story, under the name Mark Twain, "scooped" other newspapers. It was the first report of the disaster.

BECOMING FAMOUS

Sam returned to San Francisco in August 1866. Mark Twain's Hawaii articles for the *Sacramento Union* had been printed in other newspapers. People across the country were beginning to recognize the name Mark Twain. Few people knew it was Sam Clemens's pen name.

Public lectures, or speeches, were a popular form of entertainment. Sam decided to give a talk about his Hawaiian trip to make some quick money. He rented a hall and printed a handout advertising the event. The ad said that a splendid orchestra, wild beasts, magnificent fireworks, and a grand torchlight procession—would NOT be appearing. The ad ended with the line "Doors open at 7 o'clock. The Trouble to begin at 8 o'clock."

As he walked on stage, Sam had an attack of stage fright. Somehow, he managed to shuffle to the platform and begin to read his lecture. He began to

Sam began giving lectures after he returned from Hawaii.

speak in his serious "long talk." Minutes later, the audience was in awe of Mark Twain. He told them all about the wonders of the Sandwich Islands. He used words to paint funny descriptions of people and events. His way of speaking was entertaining and moving. At the end of his talk, the audience clapped wildly.

Here was an easy career! Happy with his success and the money he raked in, Sam repeated his lecture. He spoke a dozen times in cities in the West. Then he moved on to the Midwest. Finally, he filled the Great Hall of Cooper Union in New York City. The rave reviews of his lecture made Mark Twain one of the new stars of the traveling lecture circuit.

In May 1867, Mark Twain published his first book—*The Celebrated Jumping Frog of Calaveras County and Other Sketches.* One of the stories was about Jim Smiley's frog. Twain's unique humor made him famous across the nation.

A few months later, the San Francisco paper *Alta California* hired Mark Twain to be a traveling writer. The paper was sending him to Europe and the Middle East for five months. In the Middle East, Sam would visit sites of the Holy Land that were important to Christians. The trip was being organized by Plymouth Church in Brooklyn, New York. The whole journey had a religious theme. But Sam Clemens wasn't a very religious man.

TRAVELING ABROAD

Sam Clemens sailed from New York to Europe on the steamship *Quaker City.* He found out that his traveling companions for the next five months were middle-aged church members on a religious cruise. They were dignified. They didn't drink. Into this group came Sam, with his rough frontier humor. He'd brought two cases of champagne and a large supply of cheap cigars with him. On the first night of the cruise, Mark Twain reported that the passengers' idea of fun was to hold a prayer meeting. His idea of fun was to play cards or go dancing.

During the trip, Twain wrote about the sights of Europe and the Holy Land with humor. He gave his readers a fresh look at that part of the world. Sam noted everything. He listened with delight to the many new languages he heard. He even admitted that maybe he should enjoy being with the rich people on the cruise. They might help him refine his style.

While on board, Sam found at least two passengers he liked. One was Mary Fairbanks. She was the wife of the owner of the *Cleveland Herald*, an Ohio newspaper. He saw in Mrs. Fairbanks someone who would willingly help him learn better manners. He began to call her Mother, and she called him her cub. She was also a journalist and gave Sam advice on improving his writing, as well as his manners.

Mrs. Fairbanks knew the family of another passenger on board. Seventeen-year-old Charley Langdon came from Elmira, New York. Mary drew Sam and Charley into her social circle. Charley was traveling to expand his knowledge of the world before he took over the family's successful coal business. Some time during the trip, Charley showed Sam a small portrait of Charley's older

This miniature painting of Olivia Langdon captured Sam's heart.

sister Olivia. Sam saw a pretty and rich young woman. But he also saw an intelligent and educated person. She might measure up to his ideal of the perfect wife. Sam Clemens had been a wanderer since leaving Hannibal at the age of seventeen. At the age of thirty-one, it was time to think about settling down.

CHAPTER

6

A GOLDEN LIFE

(Above)
This photo
of Sam was
taken in
1867, the
same year
he met
Olivia.

IN 1867, A FEW OF THE *Quaker City* passengers met in New York City. Charley Langdon brought along his sister Olivia and his father, Jervis Langdon. One night, Sam Clemens ate dinner with the Langdons. Afterward, they went to hear the famous British author Charles Dickens read from his works. By the time the evening was over, Sam's fate was sealed. He had fallen in love with Olivia. Forty years later, he said, "From that day to this she has never been out of my mind."

ANOTHER BOOK

Mark Twain's letters from the *Quaker City* cruise were printed in the *Alta California* and in two New York papers. Elisha Bliss read them. He owned the American Publishing Company in Hartford, Connecticut. Bliss wrote Sam. He wanted to know if Sam would consider allowing Bliss to print a collection of Mark Twain's letters in a book. Bliss's firm sold books by subscription. His door-to-door salesmen sold the subscriptions before the books were published. These advance sales determined how many copies of a book would be printed. Authors received their payments based on the price of the book. The larger the number of subscriptions, the more money the author would earn. Sam liked the idea very much. He decided to call the book *The Innocents Abroad*.

Sam went to Hartford to meet Bliss and to sign the deal. While he was there, he also met Joseph Twichell. He was the minister of a new Congregational Church. The people in this church tended to be very rich. Sam had long ago stopped going to church and generally disliked preachers. But Twichell was different. Unlike the Hannibal preachers of Sam's youth, Twichell didn't try to scare or convert people. Twichell accepted people as they were. In fact, he liked Sam's sense of humor and rough manners. From their first meeting, the two men became fast friends. Sam began to think that Hartford would be an ideal place to live.

WINNING LIVY

In August, Sam visited Olivia (Livy) Langdon in Elmira, New York. Afterward he started a letter-writing campaign to win her love. He visited her several more times. During a lecture tour in Elmira, he stayed at the Langdons' house. When he asked her to marry him, Livy said yes.

Nevertheless, Livy's father had to agree. Livy had never been strong physically. Her family didn't want her to become any weaker. In those days, rich fathers gave permission for their daughters to marry. Mr. Langdon was not likely to let his daughter marry

IT'S A FACT!

Livy saved nearly two hundred of Sam's letters to her. They are in a collection of Mark Twain papers at the University of California in Berkeley, California.

Sam without checking out what he was really like. Sam kept lecturing in the East. He wrote to Livy about literature, religion, and philosophy. He begged her to educate and improve him.

At the same time, Mr. Langdon wrote to Sam's friends. He wanted to know their opinion of Sam. They all said he was a man with serious faults. He then asked Sam to meet privately with him. "What kind of people are these?" Mr. Langdon asked, pointing to the letters. "Haven't you a friend in the world?" "Apparently not," gulped Sam. Then Mr. Langdon surprised Sam by saying, "I'll be your friend, myself. Take the girl. I know you better than they do."

Once again, Sam set out on a lecture tour. In May, the proofs (first prints) of *The Innocents Abroad* came from his publisher to be checked. Sam went to Elmira and spent happy hours with Livy. They read the proofs and made plans for their future.

Sam found that Livy was a gifted editor, even though her spelling was terrible. He realized that Livy could help him improve his writing. She could help him develop a smoother style. He believed this style would appeal to more people. More readers also meant more money.

Sam *(center)* met two other American humorists, Josh Billings *(left)* and Petroleum V. Nasby *(right)* in 1869 while he was on a lecture tour.

Lecturing continued to pay well. But after he was married, Sam wanted to stay in one place and write for newspapers or magazines. His rich future father-in-law wanted to make life easy for his daughter. He loaned Sam money to buy part ownership of a New York newspaper called the *Buffalo Express.* Sam and Livy would move to

Buffalo. In Buffalo, Livy would not be too far from her family in Elmira. Sam could get back to working as a newspaperman, while he also earned money from owning the *Express*.

GETTING MARRIED

After finishing a hard lecture tour, Sam went to Elmira. By this time, he had a lot of money. Some of it came from the great sales of *The Innocents Abroad*. He was not just a funny storyteller anymore. Sam had become a best-selling author named Mark Twain.

On February 2, 1870, Joseph Twichell married Samuel Clemens and Livy Langdon in the Langdons' parlor. The next day, the couple and all the guests got on a private train car and headed for Buffalo, New York. Sam had asked friends to rent rooms for the couple while he and Livy looked for a house there. A sleigh met the newlyweds at the Buffalo train station. They enjoyed a long drive through the snow. At last, the sleigh pulled up in front of a grand house on Buffalo's finest street. When the door opened, all the wedding guests stood inside. They welcomed Sam and Livy to their new home.

Sam didn't know what to say. "Don't you understand?" Livy asked. "It is ours, all ours—everything—a gift from father." The gift included the services of a cook and a housemaid, as well as a horse and carriage. Livy's father had also hired a coachman. Livy, of course, had been in on all the planning. From that moment on, Sam put her in charge of their family life.

The first few months in Buffalo were perfect. But in the spring, doctors told Livy's father that he had cancer. His health worsened, and he died in August 1870. At the same time, Livy was pregnant.

Sam and Livy's house in Buffalo, New York

After her father's death, she had a nervous breakdown. She could sleep only with the help of strong medicine. Sam cared for her constantly.

In October, Livy almost lost the baby. A month later, she gave birth early. They named their tiny boy Langdon. The baby was probably harmed by medications given to his mother during pregnancy. With careful nursing, Langdon clung to life. When Langdon was only three months old, Livy caught typhoid fever and nearly died.

The stress of those months took a heavy toll on Sam Clemens. He grew to hate Buffalo. When the terrible winter of 1870–1871 ended, he and Livy decided to leave. They put their house and the newspaper up for sale. They spent the summer near Elmira, New York, with Livy's sister Susan Crane. Susan and her household nursed Livy and the baby.

THE HANDSOMEST TOWN

During this time, Sam and Livy decided to move to Hartford, Connecticut. Mark Twain's publisher, Elisha Bliss, was there, and so was Sam's friend Joseph Twichell. Livy also had friends in Hartford. Their grand houses were in a parklike area called

IT'S A FACT!

Two of Hartford's main businesses were the Colt factory and the Hartford insurance company. Colt made weapons of all kinds. The Hartford insured people against fire damage to their property.

Nook Farm. She knew one of the houses was for rent. It would suit them perfectly until they could build their own. Their neighbors and friends would be the town's leaders.

"Hartford," Mark Twain wrote, "is the best built and handsomest town I have ever seen. . . . They have the broadest, straightest streets . . . that ever led a sinner to destruction." He was impressed by Hartford's wealth and big businesses. The town had large insurance companies, the subscription publishing houses, and the Colt firearms factory.

Hartford was halfway between New York City and Boston. From here, Sam could easily reach both big cities. But Hartford didn't have the crowded feeling of either big city. Instead, it had well-planned city streets. Just outside town were fields and orchards and hills. Sam felt he could be comfortable with the people he met in Hartford.

Sam had grown up in rural Missouri at the edge of the western frontier. He often felt awkward in the cities of the eastern United States. But in Hartford, Mark Twain was a popular author. Livy's warm, generous nature made her a favorite among their neighbors. She fit right in.

During the fall, Livy managed the household move and took care of their sickly baby. She was also pregnant again. Mark Twain was rewriting the book he had started about his frontier experiences. He called it *Roughing It*. This new book sold well.

In the spring of 1872, Sam and Livy went to Elmira for the birth of their second child. On March 19, they had a healthy girl. They named her Olivia Susan and called her Susy for short. Their joy was joined with worry over little Langdon. Three months later, the sickly boy died.

NEW BOOK, NEW HOUSE

At the end of the summer, Livy went back to Hartford. But Sam needed to find ideas for another book to keep money coming in. The popularity of *The Innocents Abroad* and *Roughing It* convinced him he should try writing a travel book about England. In August, he sailed there alone.

Everybody in England, it seemed, had heard of Mark Twain and was reading his books. Sam was flattered by the attention from all levels of English society. He got invitations to fancy banquets. He met aristocrats, authors, and actors. Reporters quoted every word he spoke in public. But he found he couldn't write the book he had planned. He couldn't make fun of the wonderful English people he'd met. Making fun was what made his other travel books so popular.

Sam returned to the United States in late 1872. He wrote a book that made fun of American culture instead. The book was called *The Gilded Age*. Twain's coauthor was his neighbor Charles Dudley Warner, editor of the *Hartford Courant* newspaper.

In early 1873, Sam and Livy bought land in Nook Farm. They hired an architect to design a fancy house worthy of their social standing. Livy worked on sketches to give the architect. Sam ignored most of the planning and continued his lecture tours and other business interests.

When the builder brought in the building crew, the Clemenses left Hartford. They were going to spend nearly six months in Europe. Sam didn't want to be around during building. When the family returned in late 1873, the house was nearly finished.

By this time, Livy was pregnant again. She wanted to give birth in Elmira. She wanted to have the same female doctor who had delivered her other children. She wanted to be by her sister and mother. The Clemenses welcomed another healthy baby girl in June 1874. They named her Clara.

CREATING TOM SAWYER

That summer, Sam worked in the peaceful setting of Elmira's Quarry Farm. He sat in the comfort of a study built just for him. The small room opened on a view of hills and valleys and the Chemung River. Sam's thoughts turned to his childhood in Missouri. The memories came flooding back to him.

Mark Twain was about to write a masterpiece called *The Adventures of Tom Sawyer.* In it, the town of Hannibal became Saint Petersburg. His mother was Aunt Polly. His long-dead brother Henry became an irritating and perfect boy named Sid. His old friend Tom Blankenship was the model for Huck Finn. And the young Sam Clemens was Tom

Tom Sawyer happily loafs as a friend paints the fence for him. This 1898 illustration is by J. G. Brown.

Sawyer himself. He and his band of friends played pirates and Robin Hood. They dug for treasure and camped out on islands in the Mississippi River. He remembered his school days and his first girlfriend, Laura Hawkins. In *Tom Sawyer*, she became Becky Thatcher.

Day after day, Sam wrote. He began writing right after a hearty breakfast of steak and coffee. Sometimes he'd write as many as fifty pages. He'd stop around five o'clock. He'd return to the main house for supper. After a day of creative work, Sam felt filled with energy.

After writing, Sam joined his family. Livy and his two daughters gave him much loving attention. He read what he had written that day out loud. He listened eagerly to Livy's suggestions for improving his writing.

By summer's end, the mansion in Hartford was ready for the Clemenses to move in. They brought along their coachman, housemaids, cook, and gardener. Sam had just spent the summer remembering his Missouri boyhood. His boyhood home had been a very simple wooden house. This new house was a dramatic change.

The nineteen-room house was grand and fancy. The Clemens family was happy, and their guests felt their hospitality. Their doors were never locked,

The Clemenses' new home had plenty of room for guests.

and guests were never turned away. At Christmastime, Livy always decorated the house cheerfully to welcome those who stopped by.

Sam Clemens had grown up in poverty. Mark Twain was a famous author and entertainer. The rough westerner with only a grade-school education had become an honored member of the best literary and cultural circles of the East Coast.

CHAPTER 7

A BUSY HOUSEHOLD

IN LATE 1874, the editor of the *Atlantic Monthly* magazine asked Mark Twain to write a series of articles. Sam agreed. Then he panicked when he couldn't think of a subject. On a long walk with Joseph Twichell, Sam began to remember his days on and near the Mississippi. Twichell was immediately caught up in the story.

Sam hadn't thought that river life would be interesting to anyone. But his memories came quickly. Within ten days, Mark Twain had finished three articles for the magazine. The articles weren't simply about life on the river. They centered also on the characters he had met.

The Clemens family returned to Elmira for the summer of 1875. Sam again found peace and quiet.

Mark Twain finished writing *The Adventures of Tom Sawyer*. It was finally published in June 1876.

WRITING HUCK FINN AND MORE

Twain decided to write more about his boyhood. He used Huckleberry Finn as the storyteller. Huck, a character in *Tom Sawyer,* was based on Sam's own boyhood friend, Tom Blankenship. Sam's boyhood memories of the Blankenship family gave him more characters and ideas for his new story. The character of Pap Finn was partly based on Tom's violent father. The episode of a boy hiding a runaway slave had really happened. Tom Blankenship's older brother had helped a slave escape to freedom.

Jim was the other main character in the book. He was based on Uncle Dan'l. Dan'l was Sam's faithful childhood friend on his uncle's farm in Missouri. Sam remembered the way

IT'S A FACT!

Sam had seen children in Hartford gathering buckets of huckleberries. Until then, he said, he thought huckleberries were something like turnips. The berries gave him the name of one of his most famous characters—Huck Finn.

Uncle Dan'l spoke. And Mark Twain had no
trouble making Jim use Uncle Dan'l's way of
speaking. Real people whom Sam knew also
helped with Jim's character. John T. Lewis was an
African American farmer at Quarry Farm. George
Griffin was the Clemens's longtime butler. Sam
loved and admired both men. Jim, a slave,
becomes Twain's most noble character. Huck
helps set Jim free. Twain wrote quickly. By the

Sam wrote much of his best work in his study at Elmira,
New York.

end of the summer, he had finished the first sixteen chapters. Then suddenly, he couldn't write anymore.

Sam's publisher was asking for another book by Mark Twain. But Twain couldn't think of anything to write. In April 1878, he took his family to Europe again. During this sixteen-month stay, Sam planned to lecture and write. Joseph Twichell came for a time. Sam and Twichell went on a monthlong tour of Switzerland and Germany. Twain wrote a travel book, *A Tramp Abroad*, about the tour. The character, Mr. Harris, was based on Twichell.

The Clemens family returned to the United States in the fall of 1879. The next July, they were in Elmira when their third daughter was born. She was officially named Jane Lampton after Sam's mother, but they called her Jean. Another addition to the family that summer was twenty-four-year-old Katy Leary. She served the Clemenses as nanny, nurse, traveling companion, and personal maid.

Many other members of the household staff stayed with the Clemens family for years. Patrick McAleer was the coachman. He had started working for Sam and Livy at the beginning of their marriage. The butler, George Griffin, was a former slave. Sam said George came one day to wash windows and stayed for eighteen years. George and Patrick loved the Clemens girls. The men became their protectors and playmates.

In 1880, Mark Twain began work on a historical novel set in long-ago England. The story was about a young prince and a poor boy who looked alike and traded places. It was called *The Prince and the Pauper.* In some ways, the boys were historical versions of Tom Sawyer and Huck Finn. In the story, Twain wrote in a funny way about topics that he was interested in, such as twins and unfairness. Livy, Susy, and Clara told him it was the best writing he had ever done.

NIGHTLY STORIES

Sam made up stories for his daughters every night in the family's living room. The girls often told him he must include small objects that decorated the mantelpiece in his stories. He couldn't leave out a single object. But each story had to be different. Sam always had to begin his stories with the picture of a cat that was at one end of the mantelpiece. He'd continue through several figurines and vases. Then he'd end the story with the painting of a young girl they called Emmeline.

LIFE IN THE GRAND HOUSE

As Mark Twain's fame grew, life in the grand house grew more fancy. Famous visitors from many countries came. They stayed for long visits because of the Clemenses' warm welcome and their rich lifestyle. Livy finally begged Sam not to invite everyone he met to visit him in Hartford, because they always came.

The Clemenses' dinner parties had spectacular menus. Visitors ate oysters, duck, and roast beef.

Sam and his daughter Susy wear costumes and entertain their friends. Sam liked to perform.

The Clemens family in the mid-1880s (from left to right): Clara, Livy, Jean, Sam, and Susy. The dog's name is Hash.

They drank champagne and expensive wine. They enjoyed ice cream and chestnut pudding. During dinner, Mark Twain performed. He walked around the table, waving his napkin and telling stories. He often entertained the guests on the piano afterward. He sang hymns in his warm, rich voice. His stories and songs moved them to laughter or tears. After dinner parties or on Friday nights, Sam and his friends climbed to the third-floor billiard room. They smoked so many cigars that they turned the air hazy with smoke. They shot balls around the family's kittens that often played on the pool table.

Mark Twain found it almost impossible to do any steady writing in his busy household. At the age of two, Jean caught scarlet fever. Suddenly, her health caused everyone great concern. The constant worry and nonstop activity made it hard for Twain to concentrate.

He tried writing in a room in his carriage house. Then he went up the street to the Twichells' house. Finally, he moved his desk to the third-floor billiard room. He tried again and again to write.

FAILED PRINTING INVENTIONS

Sam's household expenses were going up all the time. He tried many ways to earn extra money quickly. For example, as a former printer, he was fascinated by inventions that were supposed to improve the printing industry. He put money into a process called the Kaolotype. It failed. He also invested even more money in an automatic typesetting machine called the Paige Compositor. It failed too.

He didn't have much luck. He found that he had the most success during the quiet summers in Elmira. In the peaceful study at Quarry Farm, Twain did most of his book writing.

HOME TO HANNIBAL

In the spring of 1882, Sam desperately needed inspiration for his writing. He spent six weeks traveling along the Mississippi River. He went to see Hannibal for the first time in fifteen years. To Sam, it seemed that "everything was changed in Hannibal—but when I reached Third or Fourth street the tears burst forth, for I recognized the mud."

This experience gave him enough to write a new book. He wrote *Life on the Mississippi.* Then, after seven years of trying, he finished *Adventures of Huckleberry Finn.* "I haven't had such booming working-days for many years," he wrote joyfully to his mother and Orion.

Hoping to increase his profits, Sam started his own publishing company. He put his nephew, Charles Webster, in charge of the publishing house. Charles was the son-in-law of Sam's sister Pamela. In 1885, *Adventures of Huckleberry Finn*

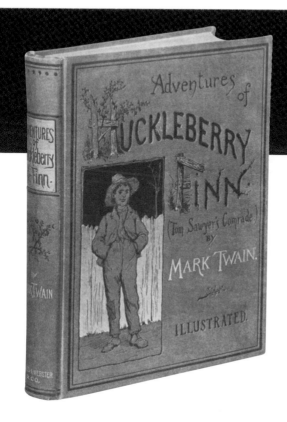

This is a first edition of *Adventures of Huckleberry Finn*.

became the company's first book. The company also later published the memoirs of the Civil War general and former U.S. president, Ulysses S. Grant.

To make money, Sam set up another long speaking tour. He invited the writer George Washington Cable to be on the tour. Mark Twain had designed a new kind of program. He and Cable would read from and would act out their stories. Known as the "Twins of Genius," Twain and Cable gave 104 performances, traveled 10,000 miles (16,000 kilometers), and stayed in hotel rooms in seventy cities. Before the tour ended, Sam grew very homesick. He fought with Cable. He got angry when he thought people expected him "to paint himself striped and stand on his head every fifteen minutes." In spite of his anger, Sam earned a lot of money.

Sam and George Washington Cable *(right)* **made a speaking tour together.**

IT'S A FACT!

Beginning in the 1960s, the actor Hal Holbrook has performed in a one-man show called *Mark Twain Tonight.* He shows *(right)* how the cigar-smoking Twain might have looked and sounded to the audiences who paid to hear him lecture. Holbrook has performed the show more than two thousand times.

One person who loved Mark Twain dearly was his eldest daughter, Susy. In 1885, at the age of thirteen, Susy began to write a biography of her father. Twain was almost fifty. Her youthful honesty flattered and delighted him. "He is a very good man," Susy wrote, "and a very funny one; he has got a temper, but we all have in this family. He is the loveliest man I ever saw, or ever hope to see."

Sam enjoyed dressing fashionably.

Fresh Challenges

Twain's next book was *A Connecticut Yankee in King Arthur's Court*. Published in 1889, it was a science fiction story about a Hartford mechanic who is struck on the head and wakes up in King Arthur's England. The public didn't quite know what to make of the book. It had humor and made fun of

English kings and queens. The book talked about long-ago warfare and modern technology. American readers generally liked it. Readers in England, on the other hand, were offended.

That same year, nine-year-old Jean began having blackouts and seizures that caused sudden behavior changes. Her desperate parents tried to find cures. The next year, in 1890, Susy left home to go to college in Pennsylvania. Her departure was hard for both father and daughter. Sam visited Susy as often as he could.

It's a Fact!

Doctors later said that Jean had epilepsy. This disease of the brain can cause a person to black out or to behave out of character.

That autumn, both Sam's mother and Livy's mother died. About the same time, doctors told Livy she had a heart disease that would slow her down. Sam developed a harsh pain in his right arm. He had to teach himself to write left-handed or stop writing altogether.

By June 1891, Sam was facing terrible money problems. He didn't have enough money to pay for their lifestyle. He had to stop the constant outflow of money as the Clemens family hosted guest after guest. He and Livy closed the costly Hartford house. They decided to take the family to Europe. There, they could save money by living in rented houses or hotels.

Livy could hardly bear to leave her beloved house with all its wonderful memories. The carriage arrived to take them to the train station. She went back into the house, saying a silent good-bye to the home she might never see again.

8

MOVING ON

(Above)
Sam and his daughter Susy walk on the deck of a steamship during their trip to Europe.

IN 1891, SAM AND LIVY took eleven-year-old Jean with them to Aix-les-Bains, France. They hoped the sulfur baths there would improve her health. Livy's sister Susan Crane was with them and so was their faithful servant Katy Leary. Nineteen-year-old Susy and seventeen-year-old Clara studied French in

Geneva, Switzerland. Then the whole family reunited for the winter in Berlin, Germany.

By this time, Mark Twain was so famous that he was recognized wherever he went. Even the German ruler Kaiser Wilhelm II was a fan. When the Kaiser invited Twain to dinner, Jean was amazed. "Why, papa," she said, "if it keeps on going like this, pretty soon there won't be anybody left for you to get acquainted with but God."

By the 1890s, Sam was well known throughout the world.

FAMILY SHOCKS

During the next two years, Sam made four trips back to the United States from Europe. He had to take care of his rapidly declining business affairs. In 1894, a rich friend named Henry H. Rogers advised Sam to give up his publishing house and to declare bankruptcy. Sam knew this step was the only way to get out of debt.

Sam and Livy were determined to pay back every dollar of the money they owed. Sam was fifty-nine years old. Livy was not well. But they decided to go around the world on another lecture tour. They would use the earnings to pay off their debt. Clara would go with them.

Before beginning the exhausting tour, the family gathered for a happy summer in Elmira. At the end of the summer, Sam, Livy, and Clara said good-bye to

IT'S A FACT!

Bankruptcy is a legal document that says a person has run out of money. A court decides how to pay off the person's debts. Sometimes a person's property is sold to make money. Sometimes the bankrupt person pays off the debts over time. This is how Sam got out of bankruptcy.

Susy and Jean. The two girls would stay with Aunt Susan and Katy Leary in Elmira. Susy went with her parents to the train station and stood on the platform waving to them until the train was out of sight.

The tour began in Cleveland, Ohio. Mark Twain performed in front of huge audiences all the way to the West Coast He thoroughly enjoyed himself. Livy, too, seemed to thrive. In September 1895, they sailed for Australia. They then went on to New Zealand, India, and South Africa. Mark Twain had become a star on several continents. Sam arrived in England in July 1896, with most of his debts paid.

Susy, Jean, and Katy Leary planned to join Sam, Livy, and Clara in England in mid-August On the day they were expected, Sam and Livy got a letter. It said Susy had fallen ill. Sam and Livy felt that something was terribly wrong. Livy and Clara sailed for the United States. Sam was sitting alone three days later when a message was handed to him. "Susy was peacefully released today," it said.

At the age of twenty-four, Susy had died of a disease called spinal meningitis. She died in the family's Hartford house. Susy had asked friends to take her there during her final days. Sam and Livy were devastated with grief. It took nearly two years before the darkness of grief lifted. During that time, Sam wrote as a way to keep his sanity. Livy hung on to life for Sam, even as her own health got worse.

> **IT'S A FACT!**
>
> **Meningitis is a serious, sometimes fatal disease. It is an infection that attacks the brain. Not much was known about the disease or how to fight it when Susy got meningitis.**

The family spent much of that time in Vienna, Austria. Mark Twain again found himself the focus of an adoring public. Their hotel rooms attracted rich, famous, and curious visitors. Mark Twain was recognized everywhere. Reporters asked his opinion on every subject. He became the star of Vienna.

FAME AND TRAGEDY

Sam's debts were paid. Money poured in from the sale of his books. By March 1898, he had regained his old spirit. In October 1900, he returned with Livy, twenty-seven-year-old Clara, and twenty-one-year-old Jean to a hero's welcome in New York. Americans thought of Mark Twain as the country's most honored writer. Twain's books captured a worldwide audience. Sales of his books soared.

The family thought about moving back to Hartford. But the town had changed since the family had been overseas. Many of Sam and Livy's friends had died or moved away. The big house reminded them of Susy. So the Clemens family settled in New York City. They enjoyed the company of friends, financial advisers, and publishers. But

Sam returned to the United States and settled in New York City in 1900.

Livy's health became much worse. Her doctors recommended that the family move to Italy, which had a warmer climate.

After a steady decline, Livy died in Florence, Italy, in 1904. Sam ached with loneliness. But he knew Livy's death had released her from more suffering. Jean once more began to have seizures. Clara had a nervous breakdown. Twain sadly returned to the United States to live in a house on Fifth Avenue in New York City.

In 1905, Sam Clemens turned seventy. His publishers invited two hundred guests to a banquet in New York in his honor. It was a celebrity night for the rich and famous. A forty-piece orchestra played. Champagne and brandy flowed. For five hours, famous people made speeches about the famous author Mark Twain.

Two years later, Sam received an even greater honor and more world attention. England's Oxford University awarded him an honorary college degree. Sam came to the ceremony dressed in a red and gray robe. Oxford's students roared with approval as he stood to receive the honor. Afterward, cheering crowds walked with him through the streets of the city of Oxford.

MORE FAMOUS

At Oxford that day, thirty other men got honorary degrees with Mark Twain. But he was so famous that they weren't given much attention. The other famous men included the British author Rudyard Kipling. The French composer Camille Saint-Saëns was honored. So was the French sculptor Auguste Rodin, whose most famous statue is *The Thinker*. Sam even outshone the brother of Britain's King Edward VII and Britain's prime minister!

The Thinker, by Auguste Rodin

Mark Twain said he'd have gone to Mars for the honorary degree he received from Oxford University in 1907.

It seemed that the people had eyes only for Mark Twain. *Harper's Weekly* magazine called him "the most advertised man in the world."

Back in New York, Mark Twain began wearing white suits all year round. He called them his "don't-care-a-damn suits." On Sundays, he waited in the lobby of the Plaza Hotel until church services ended. Then he strolled down Fifth Avenue in his white suit. He loved the attention he got from well-dressed strangers, who tipped their hats to him. He

Sam wore his Oxford robes every chance he got, including the wedding day of Clara *(second from right)*. Joseph Twichell also attended the wedding *(far right)*.

had moved his stage personality to the busiest streets of America. He had become one of America's first worldwide celebrities.

Sam built a new mansion in Redding, Connecticut, and called it Stormfield. He tried to create the same lifestyle that he and Livy had known in Hartford. But he was increasingly lonely. He grieved for Livy and Susy. Clara was living in Europe. Jean was in and out of hospitals. Joseph Twichell no longer lived close enough to comfort him.

MARK TWAIN'S VOICE

In 1888, Sam went to the laboratory of the American inventor Thomas A. Edison. Edison made several recordings of Mark Twain speaking. A fire later destroyed the records. In 1904, Twain's voice was recorded on a wax cylinder. Heat later melted the cylinder. Mark Twain was filmed in 1909 by Edison's studio. Unfortunately, this was before the days of "talking pictures," so we still don't know what Sam's voice sounded like.

HEADING OUT

Sam's health began to fail. Doctors said his chest pains were signs of heart disease. Even so, he continued smoking cigars and leading a busy social life. He dictated his autobiography to a young writer, Albert Bigelow Paine.

Sam returned from a vacation in December 1909 to spend Christmas at Stormfield. Clara had married the pianist Ossip Gabrilowitsch that fall and moved to Europe. Jean was with her father at Stormfield. She busily wrapped gifts and decorated the house as elaborately as her mother had done in Hartford. On Christmas Eve, Sam kissed his daughter goodnight and went to his bedroom. Early Christmas morning, Sam was awakened by a frantic Katy Leary. Jean was dead! She had probably died of a heart attack.

Sam watched from a window as a wagon carried Jean's coffin away. The wagon headed through a heavy snowstorm to the train that would take her to Elmira. She was buried next to Livy, Susy, and her infant brother, Langdon.

With no family left at Stormfield, Sam sought comfort again in travel. Just a few months later, in April, he returned home. Earlier in 1910, Sam had noted that Halley's Comet was scheduled to be seen again that year. Its last appearance had been when Sam was born in 1835. As the sun set on April 21, 1910, he died. On that day, the comet had just passed by and was heading out for uncharted territory.

IT'S A FACT!

Halley's Comet appears about every seventy-six years. After 1910, the comet appeared in 1986. Its next passage will be in early 2062.

GLOSSARY

apprentice: a person who is learning a trade or craft from a more experienced person

fathom: a measurement of water depth that equals 6 feet (1.8 meters)

Holy Land: areas in present-day Israel that are important to the religions of Judaism, Christianity, and Islam

justice of the peace: a person who judges cases in a local court and has the legal authority to marry people

lead line: a long rope with a lead weight at its end. The weight sits at the bottom of a river. Equally spaced colored cloths were tied on the rope. The distance between two cloths was a fathom. By seeing how many cloths were underwater, the person holding the lead line could see how many fathoms deep the water was.

Nevada Territory: a piece of land in what became the U.S. state of Nevada. The U.S. government set up the territory in 1861, and it joined the Union as a state in 1864.

the North: in the United States, the states that fought against the Confederacy (or South) in the Civil War (1861–1865)

Oxford University: a group of schools set up in the city of Oxford, England

panning: looking for gold by rinsing dirt in a pan. The person panning hopes to find gold, which will sink to the bottom of the pan after the lighter dirt has floated away.

Pony Express: a mail service. A series of riders carried the mail on horseback from Missouri to California. The Pony Express service started in April 1860 and lasted until October 1861.

the South: in the United States, the states that fought against the Union (or North) in the Civil War (1861–1865)

SOURCE NOTES

7 Mark Twain, *Chapters from My Autobiography* (New York: Harper & Brothers, 1906), 9: 6.

14 ITwain, *Chapters from My Autobiography*, 13: 452.

17 Twain, *Chapters from My Autobiography*, 8: 456.

18 Twain, *Chapters from My Autobiography*, 5: 839.

20 Dixon Wecter, *Sam Clemens of Hannibal* (Boston: Houghton, Mifflin, 1952), 58.

22 Mark Twain, *Life on the Mississippi* (Boston: James R. Osgood, 1883) 65.

22 Ibid.

23 Albert Bigelow Paine, ed., *Mark Twain's Autobiography* (New York: Harper & Brothers), 1: 308.

27 Paine, *Mark Twain's Autobiography*, 2: 282.

28 Wecter, *Sam Clemens of Hannibal*, 258.

36 Twain, *Life on the Mississippi*, 79.

38 Ibid., 111.

48 Albert Bigelow Paine, *The Adventures of Mark Twain* (New York: Grosset & Dunlap, 1944), 123.

53 Mark Twain, *Roughing It* (Hartford: American Publishing, 1872), 534, 537.

60 Paine, *Mark Twain, a Biography,* 1: 353.

63 Paine, *Mark Twain's Autobiography*, 1: 110–11.

66 Paine, *The Adventures of Mark Twain,* 181.

68 Mark Twain, "A Glimpse of Hartford," *Alta California,* March 3, 1868.

82 Twain, *Chapters from My Autobiography*, 4: 45.

83 Albert Bigelow Paine, ed., *Mark Twain's Notebook* (New York: Harper & Brothers, 1935), 163.

83 Albert Bigelow Paine, *Mark Twain's Letters* (New York: Harper & Brothers, 1917), 1: 434.

85 Henry Nash Smith and William Gibson, eds., *Mark Twain- Howells Letters: the Correspondance of Samuel L. Clemens and William D. Howells, 1872–1910* (Cambridge: Harvard University Press, 1960), 1: 215.

86 Twain, *Chapters from My Autobiography*, 4: 709.

91 Twain, *Chapters from My Autobiography*, 14: 562.

98 Justin Kaplan, *Mr. Clemens and Mark Twain,* (New York: Simon & Schuster, 1974), 382.

SELECTED WRITINGS OF MARK TWAIN

Works by Mark Twain can be found under three different names: Clemens, Samuel; Twain, Mark; and Mark Twain. The year at the end of each entry is the year the book was originally published. Modern editions can be found at your library.

The Celebrated Jumping Frog of Calaveras County and Other Sketches, 1867.

The Innocents Abroad, 1869.

Roughing It, 1872.

The Gilded Age, 1874.

Sketches, New and Old, 1875.

The Adventures of Tom Sawyer, 1876.

A Tramp Abroad, 1880.

The Prince and the Pauper: A Tale for Young People of All Ages, 1881.

Life on the Mississippi, 1883.

Adventures of Huckleberry Finn, 1885.

A Connecticut Yankee in King Arthur's Court, 1889.

Tom Sawyer Abroad, 1894.

The Tragedy of Pudd'nhead Wilson and the Comedy of Those Extraordinary Twins, 1894.

Personal Recollections of Joan of Arc, 1896.

Following the Equator and Anti-Imperialist Essays, 1897, 1901, 1905.

Chapters from My Autobiography, 1906–1907.

Extract from Captain Stormfield's Visit to Heaven, 1909.

Speeches, 1910.

SELECTED BIBLIOGRAPHY

Andrews, Kenneth R. *Nook Farm: Mark Twain's Hartford Circle.* Cambridge, MA: Harvard University Press, 1950.

Ayres, Alex, ed. *The Wit & Wisdom of Mark Twain.* New York: Harper & Row, 1987.

Clemens, Clara. *My Father: Mark Twain.* New York: Harper & Bros., 1931.

Clemens, Susy. *Papa: An Intimate Biography of Mark Twain.* Charles Neider, ed. Garden City, NY: Doubleday, 1985.

Gribben, Alan, and Nick Karanovich, eds. *Overland with Mark Twain: James B. Pond's Photographs and Journal of the North American Lecture Tour of 1895.* Elmira, NY: Center for Mark Twain Studies at Quarry Farm, 1992.

Howells, William Dean. *My Mark Twain: Reminiscences and Criticisms.* New York: Harper, 1910.

Kaplan, Justin. *Mark Twain and His World.* New York: Simon & Schuster, 1974.

Kaplan, Justin. *Mr. Clemens and Mark Twain.* New York: Simon & Schuster, 1966.

Lawton, Mary. *A Lifetime with Mark Twain: The Memories of Katy Leary, for Thirty Years His Faithful and Devoted Servant.* New York: Harcourt, Brace & Co., 1925.

Mark Twain's Letters, vols. 1–4, 1853–1871, University of California at Berkeley: 1988, 1990, 1992, 1995.

Mark Twain's Notebooks and Journals, vols 1–3, 1855–1891, University of California at Berkeley, 1975, 1979.

Meltzer, Milton. *Mark Twain Himself.* New York: Thomas Y. Crowell, 1960.

Paine, Albert Bigelow. *The Adventures of Mark Twain* (New York: Grosset & Dunlap, 1944.

Paine, Albert Bigelow, ed. *Mark Twain, a Biography.* 2 vols. New York: Harper & Brothers, 1912.

Paine, Albert Bigelow, ed. *Mark Twain's Letters.* 2 vols. New York: Harper & Brothers, 1917.

Paine, Albert Bigelow, ed. *Mark Twain's Notebook.* New York: Harper, 1935.

Paine, Albert Bigelow, ed. *Mark Twain's Speeches.* New York: Harper, 1910.

Powers, Ron. *Dangerous Water, a Biography of the Boy Who Became Mark Twain.* New York: Basic Books, 1999.

Salsbury, Edith Colgate, ed. *Susy and Mark Twain: Family Dialogues.* New York: Harper & Row, 1965.

Skandera-Trombley, Laura. *Mark Twain in the Company of Women.* Philadelphia: University of Pennsylvania Press, 1994.

Smith, Henry Nash, and William M. Gibson, eds. *Mark Twain-Howells Letters: The Correspondence of Samuel L. Clemens and William D. Howells, 1872–1910.* Cambridge, MA: Harvard University Press, 1960.

Wecter, Dixon. *The Love Letters of Mark Twain.* New York: Harper, 1949.

Wecter, Dixon. *Sam Clemens of Hannibal.* Boston: Houghton, Mifflin, 1952.

Wecter, Dixon, ed. *Mark Twain's Letters to Mrs. Fairbanks.* San Marino, CA: Huntington Library, 1949.

FURTHER READING AND WEBSITES

Arnold, James R. *The Civil War.* Minneapolis: Twenty-First Century Books, 2005.

Arnold, James R., and Roberta Wiener. *River to Victory: The Civil War in the West, 1861–1863.* Minneapolis: Twenty-First Century Books, 2002.

Gelletly, Leeanne. *Harriet Beecher Stowe: Author of Uncle Tom's Cabin.* New York: Chelsea House Publishers, 2001.

Jarnow, Jesse. *The Adventures of Huckleberry Finn and Race in America.* New York: Rosen Central Primary Sources, 2004.

Kerrod, Robin. *Asteroids, Comets, and Meteors.* Minneapolis: Lerner Publications Company, 2000.

LaDoux, Rita C. *Missouri.* Minneapolis: Lerner Publications Company, 2002.

Mark Twain Birthplace State Historical Site
http://www.mostateparks.com/twainsite.htm
The house in which Mark Twain was born is inside a modern museum in Mark Twain State Park.

The Mark Twain House and Museum
http://www.marktwainhouse.org/
Dedicated to Twain's Hartford, Connecticut, home. Contains biographical information on Mark Twain, information about the Hartford house, and information regarding the Mark Twain museum. Visitors to the website can view current exhibitions, book tours, check the latest news, and much more!

Mark Twain's Boyhood Home and Museum
http://www.marktwainmuseum.org/
A historic district includes the boyhood home at 206 Hill Street, the Becky Thatcher House, and Marshall Clemens's law office.

Mark Twain Scrapbook
http://www.pbs.org/marktwain/scrapbook/
Inspired by Mark Twain's love of scrapbooks, this website contains an interactive collection of his writings and speeches. The collection of words and pictures is arranged in a timeline of his life.

Meadows, James. *Slavery: The Struggle for Freedom.* Chanhassen, MN: Child's World, 2001.

Riddle, John. *The Pony Express.* Broomall, PA: Mason Crest Publishers, 2003.

Schott, Jane A. *Abraham Lincoln.* Minneapolis: Lerner Publications Company, 2002.

Steamboats and Paddlewheelers
http://www.steamboats.org
This site is dedicated to steamboats, past and present. Its contents include historical information, photos and videos, model building, a message board, and much more! It hosts a book of the month, as well as a web directory of other steamboat sites.

INDEX

PHOTO ACKNOWLEDGMENTS

The images in this book are used with permission of: The Mark Twain Project, The Bancroft Library, pp. 4, 31, 39, 58, 64, 98; Courtesy of the Library of Congress, pp. 6, 30 (LC-USZ62-11314), 47 (LC-DIG-ppmsc-02669), 50, 60 (LC-USZ62-28851), 74 (Memory Project, HABS, CONN, 2-HARF, 16-9); Mark Twain House & Museum, Hartford, CT, pp. 9, 32, 55, 72, 77, 80, 81, 84, 85, 91, 99; Frances F. Palmer/Currier & Ives, Publisher: A Midnight Race on the Mississippi. Colored lithograph. 1860. Museum of the City of New York. Harry T. Peters Collection, 58.300.24, p. 21; © North Wind Picture Archives, p. 26; The Mariners' Museum, Newport News, VA, p. 40; Nevada Historical Society, pp. 17, 49; Ray Jerome Baker Collection, Bishop Museum, p. 53; The Buffalo and Erie County Historical Society, p. 66; © Bettmann/CORBIS, pp. 86, 87; © Topical Press Agency/Getty Images, p. 95; © Gala/SuperStock, p. 97.

Cover Image: Library of Congress (LC-USZ62-5513).